FREE YOURSELF, LEAVE YOUR JOB & BE YOUR OWN BOSS
A GUIDE FOR ENTREPRENEURS

by ROB CUBBON

Free Yourself, Leave Your Job and Be Your Own Boss – A Guide for Entrepreneurs
by Rob Cubbon
Published by Rob Cubbon Ltd. *robcubbon.com*
© 2015 Rob Cubbon
ISBN-13: 978-1517387099
ISBN-10: 1517387094

Contents page

July 8th, 2011: The Kennedy Space Center, Florida. USA

The Space Shuttle Atlantis sits upon the launch pad.

Attached to the shuttle are two solid rocket boosters each carrying more than 500 tons of an 11-star perforated solid propellant of ammonium perchlorate, as well as another external fuel tank carrying 700 tons of liquid oxygen and hydrogen which feeds the three main engines inside the craft itself.

The rockets fire and the shuttle lifts off.

After two minutes the shuttle is 28 miles above the Kennedy Space Center and the two rocket boosters separate from the craft. They parachute down to the Atlantic where they are salvaged, inspected, and recycled.

Four minutes later, it jettisons the orange external fuel tank – the belly of the beast. This huge object won't be recycled; it's intentionally sent into a tailspin so it aerodynamically disintegrates somewhere over the Pacific or Indian Oceans.

The shuttle is now 70 miles above the launch pad and yet it still needs to another push from its internal engines to escape Earth's gravitational pull.

Another four minutes and it's all over. The Space Shuttle has traveled 150 miles and is orbiting the earth.

It has reached "escape velocity."

Almost all of the liquid hydrogen, oxygen, hydrazine, monomethylhydrazine and nitrogen tetroxide that were carried in the external fuel tanks has been burned in the last ten minutes.

For the rest of the shuttle's mission and subsequent return it'll hardly need any more fuel.

If the spaceship were to go on to Jupiter and Saturn it wouldn't need nearly as much power as was just required to leave the Earth.

The energy necessary to escape the Earth's atmosphere and gravitational pull is exponentially greater than the energy needed to, quite literally, journey into the stars.

It's the same for you on your journey toward freedom. Freedom requires a bit of planning and energy, but once you have momentum, it gets a lot easier. Once you've escaped, nothing will hold you back. The sky's the limit.

And it's not that difficult. You don't have to be a NASA space scientist. You just need desire.

This book will add freedom to your life. If you want to leave your job and set up a business, this is the book for you. And if you're already on the journey, I can point you in the right direction ... towards the heavens.

Free Yourself, Leave Your Job and Be Your Own Boss: Introduction

Welcome to the exciting, hair-raising unpredictability that is your new life.

Leaving a job and joining the swelling ranks of the new entrepreneurial class will not be without its challenges, but you're OK with that.

One thing is certain: life will never be the same again.

Maybe the thought of leaving work and setting up your own business is completely new to you. Or maybe you've thought about it for years. Either way, there are some differences in your life; you don't think the same as everyone else.

When the workday finishes, your colleagues switch off their computers, go home to cook dinner and watch TV. Other people's "downtime" is your "uptime." This is when your mind is switched on.

Maybe you listen to an inspirational or entrepreneurial podcast on the journey home. You can't wait to switch on your laptop and work on your business in the evenings. At work, you have little time for your colleagues' conversations about office politics or last night's TV shows.

You wish to free yourself and leave your job and, because of this, your life is completely different. Every free hour, every free minute, even every free second is important. You don't want to waste any time at all.

You have taken your first steps to freedom. It feels good, doesn't it, to wake up with that driving sense of purpose?

Yet there's still an uncertainty on your mind. Are you on the right path? Is there a way to accelerate the process? What if you fail?

This book is your compass on the journey; the rocket fuel for your escape.

Who am I to show you the way?

I freed myself in 2008. I'd set up a website and blog in 2006 and started a graphic design business in my spare time. It took me two years to grow my business to the point I felt ready to say, "Bye bye, boss!"

Before that, I was doing very mundane print typesetting work in London, UK. I hated my job. I hated Monday mornings. I hated Sunday evenings because of the anticipation of the workweek. I hated more than 50% of my waking hours because work – and the anticipation of it – took up that much time.

I'd had no aspirations to start a business or to free myself. I'd assumed, wrongly, that you had to just accept a shitty job and a shitty life.

I was also quite old. I wasn't your typical 20-something entrepreneur; in fact, I was in my late thirties when I first started a business.

As soon as I discovered the freedom of running my own business, I wanted to tell everyone about it. But my friends and family thought I was crazy; they didn't understand because they had the traditional employment mindset.

Instead, I started documenting the progress of my business online, where I could reach people I knew I could help; people who are already searching for freedom.

Not only did this help and inspire others on their road to freedom, but it also benefitted my business in terms of website traffic, referrals, and eventually, sales.

My website is at *robcubbon.com* – check it out and let me know what you think. You can also **sign up for my free newsletter** here at: *robcubbon.com/free*.

If you subscribe, you'll get:

- Free copies of my e-books: ***How to Market Yourself Online and Starting An Online Business***
- Two MP3s about online business
- A list of my favorite online tools
- Notification of future free Kindle books and offers

If you're interested, sign up here: *robcubbon.com/free*. And if not, that's cool too!

I also have some **free video courses** on my site that could help you on your journey.

I have a free mini-course about how to earn passive income (that's making money from digital product sales where someone clicks a buy button and money ends up in your account while you're sleeping). There are also courses about WordPress website creation and email marketing – handy skills if you want to set up a business and become free.

You can get these free courses here: *robcubbon.com/freecourses*

But that's enough about me for the time being.

Maybe you're not a 40-year-old English dude with a shitty job in typesetting. Maybe you're younger or older, or maybe you're female. Maybe English isn't your first language. Maybe you have different skills, a different family background, or different responsibilities.

But the point is this: **it doesn't matter who you are. You can free yourself.**

Anyone can leave their job, work for themselves, and enjoy freedom. You just need desire.

The inspiring people you will learn from

To research this book, I interviewed several people who successfully freed themselves from employment and now live life on their own terms. They are inspiring people – talking to them raised my spirits.

They come from vastly different backgrounds. They are married and un-married, with and without kids, from rich and poor backgrounds, old and young, educated and uneducated and from all corners of the Earth.

For example, *Sriranga Ramaseshan* from Bangalore, India was from a "poor background by Indian standards." He studied hard to eventually get a well-paying job with Hewlett Packard but quit to run his own school while his wife was pregnant with their first child.

Or *June Bui*, a young woman from the Vietnamese countryside. Although she is qualified to get a decent graduate-level job, she is now committed to a life of entrepreneurship.

Or *Brian Creager*, who was living the American dream with a high six figure salary, a wife, and two children to look after. He set up a successful men's hair care product line while still at his day job.

Or *Mads Singers*, a Dane who didn't hate his good job with IBM in London, but thought he could help more people by setting up on his own consulting business.

None of them regretted the decision to free themselves. You'll find their great advice plus stories of their unique challenges and triumphs as "Freedom Case Studies" within the pages of this book. The first is coming after this chapter.

The "runway"

The best way to leave your job is to find some way of earning money from home in your spare time.

You could start a web design and development business from home; you could do translating, copywriting or editing from home; you could do consulting; you could sell products. But earning money from something other than your job while you still have a job makes freedom easier and less stressful.

It doesn't matter if it's only a small amount of money at first. It doesn't matter if it's the same work you do in your boss's office. Making money independently is empowering and breeds confidence.

This may seem hard at first, just like burning all that fuel to get your spaceship into orbit. But your "side gig" is your passion. It doesn't matter what it is. You love it.

As the months pass and you're making more and more money, you'll need to make the decision of when you say, "Boss, I quit!"

There's no magic time to do this. You'll hear this from the interviewees in this book. Some of them waited for their side gig's income to match the income from their day job. Some didn't wait that long and just went for it. Some jumped with six months' worth of savings. Some had a years' worth of money in the bank so if their business made zero money for a year, they'd still be able to pay the rent and feed themselves.

No one I talked to said they wished they'd stayed at their job longer. They're on the entrepreneurial path now with no regrets and they're not looking back.

You've just got to find some way of making money that you're good at and you enjoy. Do it in your spare time and leave work.

It's that simple. And you can do it.

Minimalism

Another way to make the runway (the length of time until your business is profitable) last longer is to cut back on expenses. This is one reason why minimalism is popular amongst entrepreneurs.

Buying only what you need to survive and cutting back on all extravagances and luxuries can be life changing.

Western consumer culture pushes people to spend their entire paycheck (or more) each month. Chris Rock once said that black people spend money like it has an expiration date. But this is true of all races and cultures.

Most people spend exactly what they earn each month (some a little bit more; some a little bit less).

Think about what you've bought this year. How much was necessary for survival? When considering a purchase, ask yourself, "Do I really *need* this?"

Look at your recurring monthly expenses. Maybe you spend money on a TV subscription service, but as an entrepreneur you'll watch less TV so is that really necessary?

Iva Ursano, a freelance writer whose "Freedom Case Study" is coming next, looked at her life with a fresh perspective after coming back from volunteering in Costa Rica. She realized she was working to pay for an apartment and a car – that she needed for work. She ditched the apartment and rented a room instead, sold the car, and left work in the blink of an eye.

Minimalism is especially useful when cutting down on

unnecessary clutter in your home. There may be books, DVDs, and other items that you don't care for that can be given away or sold on eBay.

If you can stretch your minimalism to your grocery shopping you will find that raw meat and vegetables are cheaper than processed or ready meals. Eating real foods will also ensure a healthier diet.

You will also find that getting rid of possessions and cutting down on expenses will make you feel much better. Getting rid of possessions may not make you much money, but it'll result in a tidier home or workplace which will help you concentrate on growing your side gig.

So what have we learned so far?

If you're still at work this is what you need to do:

- Think of some service that people will pay you for that you enjoy and can do in your spare time (writing, editing, web design, etc.).
- Find people in your network you can provide that service to.
- Start making money.
- Spend less money.

If you haven't said these words yet: "Boss, I quit!" then please re-read the above bullet points. They may seem overly simple to you, but they are very important.

You'll notice what I haven't included in the above four bullets. I *didn't* say:

- "Spend $100 on a website design."
- "Spend $200 on targeted Facebook ads."
- "Spend ages thinking of an amazing Big Idea that no one else has ever thought of."

There's a right way and a wrong way to escape from employment. Keep reading to find out how to start. And, next up, here's our first "Freedom Case Study". Meet Iva.

Freedom Case Study:
Downsizing, freelancing, and volunteering with Iva Ursano

Iva Ursano is from Sudbury, Ontario. Sudbury is 200 miles north of Toronto. It has long, cold, snowy winters where the temperature can go down to -50°C (-58° F). That's cold.

Iva's family never encouraged her to get a higher education. The norm was to leave school, get a job, marry, and have kids.

She married, but her marriage broke down when her son was one year old. Iva found herself living off welfare, unemployed, suffering from depression and "pretty much scared out of my tree" as she explained it.

After a year, she got off welfare with a seasonal job with the Canadian government. When this work started to dry up, she studied to become a hairdresser and a few years later, a correctional worker. She worked 14-hour days both at a hair salon as well as at a homeless shelter for teenage children. After a year of that, she gave up the shelter job and continued on as a hairstylist.

In summer 2014, and after almost 20 years of hairdressing, inflammation in her shoulder was so bad that she had to receive cortisone shots to continue her job at the salon.

Feeling that she was "too young to become a pin cushion," she immersed herself in more studies, this time online, to see what the freelance writing world could offer.

Always believing she had writing talent, she wrote guest articles for some of the world's most popular personal development blogs. After only a few months of building a writing portfolio, she started getting paying jobs.

In May 2015, Iva's life changed dramatically when she volunteered for three weeks in Costa Rica. She met many people who had virtually no personal wealth but huge amounts of happiness. On returning to Canada, she set out to free herself.

She realized the only reason she was chained to the job at the salon was to pay for an unnecessary lifestyle: car, apartment, expenses, etc. So she moved out of her $1000/month apartment and sold all her belongings. She was fortunate enough to find a nice room to rent in a beautiful house from a lovely lady, which allowed her to cut her hairdressing work back to 3 days a week.

Slowly she started getting more writing clients and in July 2015, she quit her salon work completely to concentrate entirely on her online writing career. Her freelancing income is now more than her hairstyling income ever was.

She plans to continue volunteering in Costa Rica, Nicaragua, and Panama during the Canadian winters. Living a life of complete freedom, the only requirements she needs to support herself are a laptop and a Wi-Fi connection.

ivaursano.com

How to make money

Money is the ultimate paradox when it comes to entrepreneurship.

Your business will either succeed or fail depending on the money it makes. Entrepreneurs rate almost every metric in their business against the "bottom line" or profit.

Yet entrepreneurship is hardly ever about money. For most people, especially the new class of laptop entrepreneurs, freedom and the ability to create your own reality are much more common incentives.

Rather than concentrating on what makes money, it's usually better if you concentrate on what you love doing. Building a business is hard work, but it's ten times easier to work on something you love. Of course, you have to make sure doing what you love makes money.

Take me as an example. I hated my work. I detested doing typesetting for company reports. Who wouldn't? I started a design blog but I quickly "pivoted" to talk about the business of design. I loved telling other designers how to get more clients, make more money, and turn their skills into a business. I naturally wanted other people who hated their jobs to discover the same freedom I'd found. I aligned my business with a passion of mine. And that's what you've got to do – sooner or later.

Active or Passive

There are two ways your new business can make money –

actively or passively.

Active income is where you trade hours for dollars. In other words, you perform a service such as web design, accounting, or consulting. The amount you are paid depends on how much work you do. Your ability to earn more money, or "scale the business," is limited by the number of hours you work and how much you can charge. Active income is not very scalable.

Passive income is different. A business earns passive income when it sells an asset such as software, a digital training course, or a productized service. This can be scaled.

The best example of passive income scaling is with digital products. For instance, I sell video courses. Because I've already created and recorded the material, and the delivery costs are negligible, I can scale the business easily by selling more copies. I don't have to work harder or raise the price to make more money. My digital products make money while I sleep.

But before you conclude that passive income is "better" than active income I would urge caution. Passive income takes a while to get going whereas active income is easier to earn when you're starting out.

Start with active income

This won't be true for everybody, but the best way to escape your job is to offer some sort of service. The service is likely to be aligned with your interests and talents. It may even be what you are actually doing in employment.

When I was working doing mind-numbingly boring

typesetting, I got paid $40/hour. It wasn't a bad wage, until I realized the design agency was charging the client $200/hour for my time.

Working from home, I could charge clients much less and still double my hourly rate. And this is exactly what I did.

I managed to get clients through my early attempts at blogging, and the business grew through referrals and repeat customers.

I didn't dream up some life-changing app, disrupt an industry, or employ clever marketing tactics. I simply offered a service to a client base I knew I could satisfy.

While earning active income, prepare for passive income

Active income is a great way to start because you can prepare your business for passive income while you're earning.

As I mentioned, I used content marketing to get clients. I created useful blog posts that attracted people who were looking for freelance graphic designers. This served a dual purpose. It gave me web traffic *and* authority, which led to near-term clients, but it also allowed me to build an email list of interested people that I could sell products to at a later date.

I was happy running a graphic and web design business. I enjoyed doing a good job for my clients. It felt great to stay at home and make money instead of commuting to a crappy job I hated.

It also gave me the luxury of time. I used that time to build an audience and experiment with various passive income streams.

I've kept *a record of all my passive income earnings* over the years and the trajectory is really interesting.

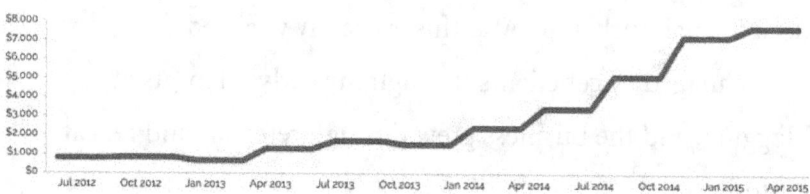

As you can see, I was earning less than $1000 passive income a month for many months. I didn't earn more than $2000 a month for years. But, during 2014, my passive income started rising quite dramatically.

In fact, in the early months of 2012, my passive income mainly came from affiliate commissions (you can earn commissions from having links to products on your site). However, the passive income increases in 2014 were mainly due to sales of my own products, particularly video courses on Udemy. (Udemy is an online education marketplace where instructors from around the world can create and sell courses on their areas of expertise.)

I tried a few different passive income ideas before finding something that worked, but in the meantime I always had the active income from my design business to fall back on.

You can find my passive income reports here: *robcubbon.com/ income-reports*

My strategy to free yourself

This is my strategy to free yourself, leave your job, and live life on your own terms:

- Work in your spare time to provide a well-paid service for clients.
- Develop and maintain a website.
- Constantly add useful information to your website which attracts more clients and grows your authority.
- Collect email addresses on your website.
- When your income from your side gig reaches a respectable level and you have 6-12 months of savings in your back pocket, **leave your job**.
- Continue to grow your active income through client work.
- Outsource and hire so you can take on more work.
- Add other passive income streams to your business without getting distracted.

This is just *my* strategy. It may not work for you. There are plenty more ideas coming up in this booklet plus more strategies from my amazing interviewees.

And don't forget these two main takeaways:

- Only leave work when you have alternative sources of income and money saved up to cover your living expenses.
- Active income is easier than passive income at first.

But what are you going to do to make money? That's what we'll address in the next chapter.

Why you don't need a Big Idea or a "niche"

You may know exactly what you want to do in your business. But most of us start out with less than a clue.

People think that they need a Big Idea. They think they've got to dream up the next Facebook or they need to secure millions in venture capital. In reality, they just need to start.

Twitter started out as a side project created by a startup that was building a podcasting platform. They didn't plan Twitter.

Another common stumbling block for entrepreneurs is choosing a "niche" for their business.

A "niche" is a specific area or position with an industry. Business gurus dictate that you should "niche down" or hone in on an ultra-specific niche so that you can more easily dominate it.

So, if you are a copywriter you could be the "auto-responder guy"; or if you are a designer you could be the "logo designer guy"; or if you are a developer you could be the "membership site guy."

As with all business advice, "niching down" is right only some of the time. Don't let this advice is stop you from getting started.

It's OK to not have a niche or a Big Idea. All you have to do is go down this easy-to-follow path: *your own way*.

You *are* your niche

Take me as an example (oh no, not again!) Who am I? I'm the "freelance-artworker-turned-graphic-designer-turned-web-designer-turned-best-selling-author-turned-online-course-creator-who-now-sometimes-blogs-about-personal-development guy."

It doesn't exactly roll off the tongue, but it works for me.

I'd get bored doing the same thing all the time. I've moved on to more interesting, more lucrative areas (for example, online course creation).

Don't get distracted from getting started

Many people postpone getting a website, postpone content creation, postpone product launches or postpone starting a business because they're thinking, thinking, thinking about their niche or their Big Idea.

This is a huge mistake. You will find your niche more easily by getting a website, creating content, launching products, and starting a business. You will find yourself inside the act of creation.

YOU WILL FIND YOURSELF INSIDE THE ACT OF CREATION.

Rob Cubbon

It will change anyway

In the beginning of 2000, WordPress, Facebook, Google AdWords, Twitter, Kindle, and iTunes didn't exist. In the next five years there will be many new life-changing apps and there will be niche businesses springing up around them. You could dominate one of them. What's the point of worrying about a niche now when there could be a more obvious one just around the corner?

In five years, our businesses and lives will look completely different than they do today. Guaranteed.

All you have to do is to make money.

Sure, some people will spend time and money building a product – and there's nothing wrong with that. But it's the hard way. You just need to provide a service that people will pay for.

What service should you provide?

That will depend on your skills and your passions. Think about something you can do that fits the following three criteria:

1. Something you love doing.
2. Something you're good at.
3. Something people will pay well for.

Everyone will be able to think of a product or service they can create that occupies this "sweet spot." It may not seem obvious to you at the moment but, if you continue to think about it and read books like this one, it'll come to you.

What topics have you always been interested in? What groups of people do you naturally associate with? What area of commerce have you spent a lot of money in? Continually think over these questions and sooner or later you'll come up with your "sweet spot."

To whom?

To whom do you sell these products or services? The easiest way to get clients and customers when you're starting out is from your professional contacts. Your network can help you get your initial side gig clients, but isn't the best long-term solution.

Over time, you should also develop an authority website with useful information on the industry you operate. You'll build trust with your readers, who will eventually become clients.

You should also take every opportunity to meet people. Go to meetups, conferences, and masterminds with business people. (More about this later.)

You can do it

You can launch your service that starts your business. Of course there will be ups and downs and mistakes and pivots along the way, which is all the more reason to start today.

Don't let anything distract you from taking action. Put that decision-making energy towards taking action in your business and your business will grow out of this action.

So, how do you take action? You make money. It's as simple as that. You get paid to provide a service to a client outside your normal 9 to 5.

This doesn't have to be doing something you absolutely love

but it does need to be at least aligned with a passion you have. For example, say you absolutely love writing and you get your first few paying gigs editing computer game instructions. Sure, you may be uninterested in computer game instructions but you will be overjoyed to be working within the industry you love.

You've just got to get the ball rolling. Once you start getting work you learn more about running a business, dealing with clients, and you get to know more about what they want and how the industry works.

So, how do you get clients? We'll come to that in the next chapter. But first, another Freedom Case Study.

Freedom Case Study: *Paying off student debt in Vietnam with Jeremy Ginsburg*

Jeremy Ginsburg was born in Minneapolis, Minnesota and studied Economics at the University of Wisconsin Madison. During his college years, he started a business transporting college students to away football games.

He hung around Madison after graduation and worked in a couple of restaurants. One of them, which served Thai/Lao cuisine, "became his kitchen" – he would eat for free and would take home the leftovers.

The entrepreneurial spirit, combined with this frugality (and selling a few items on eBay), earned him enough cash for a one-way ticket to Vietnam, plus a few months of living expenses once he got there.

In Vietnam, Jeremy worked out he could live for $1000/month but earn $1500/month teaching English. Almost immediately, he started to meet entrepreneurs – "digital nomads" who earn money from their laptops while enjoying the cheap standard of living Southeast Asia provides.

Two weeks after he started teaching English, Jeremy earned $300 editing a video for a contact he'd met in Ho Chi Minh City.

As more freelance video editing work rolled in, Jeremy was

able to pare back his teaching to only eight hours a week. Just eight hours a week was enough to cover his rent and living expenses. The rest of the time he was free to learn more about online business.

Meanwhile (here's another string to his bow) Jeremy started performing music, getting paid 1,000,000 Vietnamese Dong ($50) per night.

Eventually he stopped teaching English altogether, and focused on video production, writing, and music gigs. At the same time, Jeremy discovered he was able to live for $600/month as he moved to a cheaper apartment and gave up drinking alcohol.

Within just three years of graduating, Jeremy was able to pay off all his student debt from halfway around the world in Vietnam.

Jeremy now has a website, a YouTube channel, and many skills that people pay for. He's cleverly building a reputation, authority, and a following – preparing a solid foundation which will help him earn passive income in the future.

Entrepreneur, copywriter, videographer, musician … it's certainly hard to pigeonhole Jeremy.

Oh, and Jeremy also speaks fluent Vietnamese and has appeared on a several Vietnamese reality TV shows!

www.jeremyginsburg.com

Jeremy's parody of Gloria Gaynor's "I Will Survive"– "I Work Online" video *youtu.be/9ymMI4N9YFQ*

How to get your first five paying clients

Earning active income – performing a service for clients – is your best bet going forward. So how do you achieve this? How do you get your first five well-paying clients?

What are you going to do for them? This depends on what you're good at and what you enjoy, as we've discussed. But try to hone in on some task that is useful, needed, specific, and *something you'll perform well.*

I offered graphic design services because that was one skill I had that I knew was in demand, but this will naturally vary for you. Once you've decided on this task you need to promote yourself so people know what you're offering.

Your contacts

Your first paying clients are likely to be people you know already. Many of the people I spoke to used their existing contact list as their first port of call in looking for clients.

And just in case there's any confusion, I'm talking about professional contacts here, not friends and family – they're the worst people to work for.

Try to get contacts from your contacts. Ask former colleagues who have moved to other companies if they know anyone who might be interested in the service you're offering. The beauty of a contact list is that it's viral – even if you think you only know a few people, people know people who know people and so your reach is wider than you think.

You just need to put the word out there. And help people. Introduce two people who you think may connect well together. People will always remember you if you give them a good introduction and will naturally want to reciprocate.

Networking

You may think that "networking" is a dark art that only smarmy opportunists are good at, but it's a skill we have to exercise throughout our lives.

The best networking is done offline. A stronger connection is made when you meet someone face-to-face and that is the reason I recommend you go to as many meetups, conferences, and events as you can.

Even though conferences are expensive, connecting with and learning from relevant professionals in our industry is well worth the investment. If I walk away from a conference with just one new connection or one new idea that will help my business, I'm happy with the event.

Make helping people your primary mission when you go to these conferences and meetups. Never go to an event with an intention to pitch your services as you'll come across as pushy and 'salesy'. People will ask you what you do anyway, so there's no need.

Social media

The same rules apply in the online world as in the offline world. It's easy to make connections with people in your industry online. That's the problem: it's too easy! Don't spread yourself too thin on social media.

Concentrate only on a few groups. Help people. Connect people. Pretty soon you'll develop a reputation of expertise within a certain area.

3rd party freelance sites

I debated whether or not to include this section as I never like to advise anyone to look for work on sites like Upwork and Freelancer.com. The problem I have with them is their bidding platforms often turn into a race to the bottom on the price for your service.

You're not really running a business on these sites as you're essentially working on other people's businesses here.

Only work on these sites if you have absolutely no other way of making money and view them only as a very short-term option.

Once you've built a portfolio and client testimonials, you should be able to raise your rates and find clients elsewhere.

Website

It's most important to develop your own website – a place online that you can control. No one will take you seriously unless you have a decent website. I'll explain in a later chapter how to get one and how to create content that will attract paying clients.

You should also use a proper email – either a Gmail email with your name or an email address with your website's domain. For example, mine is rob@robcubbon.com – don't use a Yahoo, Hotmail email address or anything else or you won't be taken seriously.

What to say to your potential clients

This is a skill that will improve with experience. Try to say as little as possible to clients. Say as much as you need to and no more.

Clients are generally paying you to take pain or confusion away from their lives – so listen to the client, understand their needs, and say "I can do that."

If you agree on a price, you must confirm it in writing. You may like to draw up a proposal or download a contract online. It will depend on the job and the client.

How much do you ask for? Everyone makes the mistake of asking too little at first. Always charge at least double what you're getting at work.

There's no feeling like it

Getting your first client is an amazing feeling. You can't wait to start work.

There you are, sitting at home – making money on top of your salary. That's when you get the bug.

Freedom Case Study: *Running a business and bringing up two kids with Kelly Exeter*

Kelly Exeter, from Perth in Western Australia, got a design job straight after college. However, she often found herself freelancing for friends and family. This was *free*-lancing with emphasis on the "free" – she was building websites for people as a favor. As she built her portfolio and her network expanded, she began charging.

By word of mouth, this freelance work grew until she was too busy working for her own clients to keep working at her job. In October 2006, she sublet a tiny 10 ft. x 10 ft. office in the same building as her previous company, and Swish Design was born.

Within two months, she was earning more than her salary at her original job. Kelly's ability to "mind read" her client's wishes, her attention to detail, design skills and over-delivering meant the business grew and grew. She moved out to bigger offices and took on extra staff.

However, some of Kelly's greatest strengths – her immersion into the business and her personal attention with clients – also led to her downfall. On the day her first son was born, July 31st 2009, Kelly found herself doing the end of the month invoicing from her hospital bed.

Kelly struggled through a difficult period of running a business whilst taking care of a new baby. Although she eventually hired a nanny, the help came too late. The stress of looking after a baby, a house, and a business was too much and she had a breakdown 18 months after the birth.

Luckily, she had support from her husband, Anthony. A math teacher by day, Anthony had little design experience and had never run a company before. But his penchant for systems and processes enabled the business to work without Kelly's day-to-day involvement.

Kelly has even been able to take on another part time role as a writer and editor for Australia's foremost community for micropreneurs, *Flying Solo*.

Kelly regrets that she initially gave too much of herself to clients. Although she had hired staff, it was still her doing much of the interaction with clients and assessing their design needs; she was indispensable to the business.

It may be good to be indispensable to your employer's company but it's not good when it's your company. You need to delegate and empower other people to do what you can do so that the business can grow and ultimately run without you.

She explains her newfound philosophy as, "If teaching someone how to do a 1-minute task takes 5-minutes you should do it." Resist the temptation to do the 1-minute task yourself. Once your staff member has learned how to do that task, you'll never have to do it again – saving you hours in the future.

She also advises women to use every month of the pregnancy to plan for what's coming.

Kelly's son is now 6 years old and she and Anthony also have a 2-year-old daughter. Swish Design is still running strong.

www.swishdesign.com.au

kellyexeter.com.au

Working from home

The switch away from employment, whether sudden or gradual, will involve working from home.

Personally, I found home-working easy to get used to. I'm not a morning person and I hated my early commute in London. However, other people can't imagine getting anything done at home.

Home office

Find a quiet part of the house where you can operate away from distractions. This can be a spare room or a bedroom. All you will need is a computer and maybe some spare paper and pencils; your "home office" doesn't need to be big or fancy.

The last thing you want to do is to rush out and buy stuff for your new entrepreneurial life. We're trying to spend less, remember?

The great thing about freeing yourself and building a business today is that you can start with what you already possess – your computer, phone, and Internet connection. We are incredibly lucky to be alive at this time where businesses can be started with little or no money.

I had a corner of a spare room I turned into my home office when I started out. Years later, I changed from a desktop computer to a laptop and now my "office" can be anywhere – the local café, a hotel lobby, a beach bar … but I'll get onto location independence in a subsequent book.

Attitude

Your attitude toward your home office will vary depending on the sort of person you are.

Some people need to be strict. They wake up to an alarm clock at the same time each morning. They dress in a suit, have breakfast, and wave goodbye to their significant other as they walk away from the house only to return five minutes later to start work! These tend to be the sort of people who write books about productivity and urge others to do the same thing as it works for them.

I am on completely the other end of the scale. I'm never woken by an alarm clock. I never wear a suit. I don't have a set time to work and a set time to play. I never plan my days. I don't have a "work space" per se but, if I did, it would be a complete mess.

My attitude toward work may be too lax for some. Everything I shared about myself in the previous paragraph goes against the mainstream "wisdom" you get from books on productivity and home working.

We're all different. You have to see what works for you. But if you love running your business, you'll be able to work from home on it.

Focus

Focus is especially important for entrepreneurs as we can easily get distracted by new ideas.

To help limit distractions while I'm working, you can use tools like *Freedom.to*, which blocks social media sites, and *Inbox Pause*, which stops Gmail from notifying you of incoming email until you're ready for it.

Some people swear by the "Pomodoro" technique, where you work in 25-minute blocks separated by 5 minutes rest.

But the most important "productivity hack" of all when you're working from home is simply self-motivation. You're reading a book called *Free Yourself*, and I know your freedom is a motivating cause!

Don't let people who have never worked for themselves or people who have never worked from home put you off. Some people will look at you as if you've got two heads and tell you it's impossible. Don't listen to these people. If you are reading this book it means you have motivation.

It's not for everybody. But it's for you. You will naturally develop your own way to focus that puts you in your "flow state" where you are most productive.

Meetups

Workaholism and "entrepreneurial loneliness" are two ills that commonly afflict homeworkers. Thankfully, connecting with other entrepreneurs and people building businesses on the side is a great antidote.

Get away from your computer and into real life situations where you can mix with other entrepreneurs. Talking about business with others will result in fantastic advice, friendship, and unexpected business opportunities. It's also a great way to let off steam.

Where do you meet other entrepreneurs? I've always found *MeetUp.com* a great resource for connecting with local business people. For links to this and other resources please go here: *robcubbon.com/kindle7*

Accountabili-buddies

Online, there are tons of niche hangouts for whatever type of business you're working on. Facebook groups, Google Plus communities, LinkedIn groups – choose you poison. But don't spread yourself too thin. Social media may be great for finding like-minded souls and advice but it can also be a terrible drain on your time. Focus on one social media channel only and ignore those cute cat images!

Once you have found an individual who is on a similar path, ask them for a quick Skype call to discuss a business topic you're both passionate about.

Some of these Skype calls or relationships will be more enjoyable and productive than others. When the relationship is right you can move to the "accountabili-buddy" stage of the relationship.

How it works is both you and your new "accountabili-buddy"

set goals, certain tasks in your businesses that you would like to achieve by the time you have your second Skype chat in a week or two's time.

The value in these relationships is accountability. If you've said, "I'm gonna do this by next week," it's embarrassing to admit to your buddy that you've failed.

Fear of this embarrassment alone means you usually succeed. If you didn't succeed because you underestimated something or if you decided against it, fine. You can talk about that with your buddy – they're in a similar business as you, after all, they'll understand and find this interesting. You'll both learn from the conversation.

Masterminds

A mastermind is a group of "accountabili-buddies." They are generally groups of 4 or 5 broadly similar entrepreneurs, who meet once a week for an hour. Members of the group take turns in the "hot seat," to discuss the challenges and proposed next actions in their business.

Other members of the group ask questions and offer their input and suggestions. The whole group benefits from these discussions, since other members may be facing similar issues.

For accountability, members openly share their goals of what they'll get done before the next meeting. New projects can also be discussed – new branding, website designs, sales copy, for example, can be put up for comments. Some advice is taken; some is ignored. Discussing problems and issues in your business helps you with decision-making and clarity.

Remote masterminds can be set up very effectively on Google Hangouts. They can even be recorded for future reference. The content of the mastermind discussion is usually confidential.

"Accountabili-buddy" calls and mastermind sessions are completely free to the participants, and they usually only take around an hour a week. And yet, you can get an idea or receive guidance that could result in thousands of dollars and amazing growth for your business.

I would advise *everyone* in business or wanting to start a business to search out accountability partners, masterminds, and meet-ups. All successful entrepreneurs do this.

The benefits in terms of ideas, focus, and accountability are huge, while the costs and time commitment are negligible. Do it!

Freedom Case Study: *Utilizing the power of self-learning and networking with Mads Singers*

Mads Singers left his home in Denmark when he was 16 to study Information Technology. However, two years later, he didn't feel he was learning much and started looking for job opportunities. Mads eventually found an IT role for Xerox in Dublin, Ireland. This was August 2002. A life of IT support beckoned.

However, after only a couple of months of inspiration from his new manager, Mads' "IT dream" had turned into a dream of becoming a manager himself. As he wasn't prepared to go back to school to study management, he became obsessed with personal development in relation to management. He read every book he could get his hands on and even though people were saying, "Mads, you're good with numbers, there's no way you'll be good with people," he slowly got promoted to first leadership and then management roles.

Further career advancement took Mads to the UK to work for IBM in various people and project management roles. Despite enjoying his new role at IBM, Mads wanted to help more people so he started doing different types of volunteer work and coached and mentored people so that they enjoyed some of the amazing growth he'd experienced himself.

His job at IBM took him to different parts of Eastern Europe and Southeast Asia where he also did volunteer work. It was on one of these volunteer missions in Davao where he was introduced to "digital nomads" – location-independent online business people who can work anywhere as long as they have Wi-Fi and a laptop. He joined a private community for location independent entrepreneurs called the Dynamite Circle.

At this time he started to take on business coaching clients. The clients came from his ever-growing list of business contacts from his IBM and Xerox jobs and also new contacts from the Dynamite Circle.

Mads is different from everyone else I've interviewed for this book and different from most other entrepreneurs who left their job: Mads didn't hate his job.

Still, he was anxious to try something new. "I've always been jealous of people who'd had great challenges. I wanted to take the jump and try how it felt to be uncomfortable so I had to do amazing stuff to survive."

Mads left his well-paid comfortable corporate career, and moved to Davao in the Philippines. He had no more than $10,000 in savings, and his only income was $200/month from one client. Shortly after taking the jump, Mads attended a Dynamite Circle conference in Bangkok in October 2014 with 400 "digital nomads." His coaching skills and knowledge from

IBM of outsourcing work to the Philippines was particularly popular amongst the attendees.

Mads was booked solid and earned $10,000+ the following month – an amount that even surpassed his corporate salary. However, entrepreneurs don't have regular incomes and by January 2015, all the coaching had dried up and Mads' income had dropped drastically. This "feast and famine" cycle is something a lot of entrepreneurs will be familiar with.

In response, Mads restructured his business slightly to include the management of outsourced assistant roles in the Philippines for businesspeople who don't have the time or skills to do this. This helped him create more stabilized income, whilst enabling him to do as much as coaching as he wished.

Looking forward, Mads is keen to continue working with people and build successful businesses, while sharing what he has learned from his experience and his personal development. He doesn't believe in being tied to a certain place and wants location independence to be part of any business venture he gets involved in.

Mads said he doesn't expect to go back to a corporate job anytime soon, though he's sure there would be plenty of roles he would enjoy. "Overall my ability to prioritize my time, location and efforts based on what I want to achieve is the type of freedom that's very difficult to let go of after you've experienced it."

madssingers.com

Habits – Your family and your health

There are two important sides to your life that you have to factor into your habits as you start to work from home: your family and your health.

Let's start with family. It's clear from all the successful businesspeople I've interviewed that spousal agreement is key. You cannot do this without your significant other on board.

One of my interviewees is *Mary Shaw*, a UX project manager from Connecticut in the US. "Make sure you have your significant other's agreement," she told me. "That's critical. You have to go into this as a team."

In fact, many entrepreneurs' partners are an important part of their business – either providing support or performing essential roles within the business. An obvious example of this is the hugely successful John Lee Dumas, the founder of Entrepreneur on Fire – one of the world's most successful business podcasts. His significant other, Kate Erickson, is a content creator and community leader. She runs the business machine while John gets the ideas and hosts the show.

A clear distinction between "work time" and "play time" is also of huge importance. The work on your business never really stops. There is always more to be done and there are always ways you can improve, so you have to know when to stop each day. You have to know where the "off switch" is and this isn't always easy.

Many entrepreneurs have children and they have to work hard to make sure they aren't overlooked during transition – or any time after that.

The way to ensure you are working as a team with your family is to be in complete agreement about "family time" and "work time." Whether this is on a strict timetable or not, it is crucial that you factor in sufficient time with your family.

You will not be able to function properly as a human being without regular "down time" with your family. Don't be tempted to skimp on family time or rest time – your business, your life, and ultimately, your family will suffer if you do.

The second most important side to your life is your health.

You have to set aside time for physical exercise. Some would say three times a week is the minimum but it is better if you exercise every day.

Make it a priority to go for a half hour walk every day. Better yet, take your family with you.

Yoga and Tai Chi are great daily practices as they can be done almost everywhere – you basically only need a flat floor six foot by six foot. Any sort of physical exercise is good and you must have this habit factored into your week.

The great thing is, aside from the emotional and health benefits, family and exercise time will actually make you more productive during your work hours.

In a previous "Freedom Case Study" we met *Jeremy*

Ginsburg, who successfully paid off his student debt while working online and traveling in Vietnam. Before this, in 2012, he was diagnosed with depression but refused to take anti-depressants. Instead, Jeremy used meditation, books, healthy food, and exercise to cure it.

There are more great habits I can add to exercise and family downtime:

- **Eat healthily** – a bit of a no-brainer, but remember, proper food is often cheaper than processed fast food.
- **Drink water** – water cleanses your system; try to drink several glasses a day.
- **Sleep well** – aim for 7.5-8 hours per night.

Meditate – this is something I talk about in my first book in this series, *Free Your Thoughts: How I Re-programmed Myself For Happiness And How You Can Too.* The habit of meditation helps you in so many ways. If I didn't meditate, I wouldn't have a business.

Freeing yourself and working on your own business puts you "outside the norm." For this reason, you need to take on board many of the things I've explained in this chapter.

To summarize:

- **Don't neglect your loved ones** – ensure they are on board with your new direction.
- **Don't neglect your health** – factor in several periods of exercise during the week.
- **Expand your circle of business contacts and immediately**

set up accountability partners and/or masterminds – this is essential for keeping you focused.

- **Live frugally within your means** – only spend money on the essentials.

These above four points are essential to the success of your freedom-building business.

Freedom Case Study: *Leaving work twice with Mary Shaw*

Mary spent most of her twenties traveling the length and breadth of the USA playing college halls as a singer-songwriter. She played solo concerts at over 150 college campuses over a 6-year period from 1987-1993, covering 50,000 miles with her guitar in the back of a minivan.

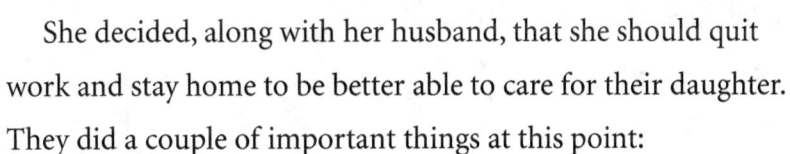

However, after getting married she settled down and worked for various companies in the Connecticut area on a variety of web and project management related roles.

Life changed suddenly in 2006 when Mary's three-year-old daughter was hospitalized with a life-threatening illness.

She decided, along with her husband, that she should quit work and stay home to be better able to care for their daughter. They did a couple of important things at this point:

1. Mary didn't quit straightaway. She gave 7 weeks notice to her employer and told everyone in her company that she was quitting and going freelance. Word definitely got around that Mary was at home with a computer, phone, and Internet connection – and was available for freelance work.

2. They had been saving money. Even if Mary didn't pick up

a dime working from home, they would have been able to cover their mortgage, health insurance, and other payments for at least 12 months.

Mary spent the next few years at home, picking up work from ex-colleagues and contacts from her previous jobs. However, the downturn after the 2008 financial crisis forced her back into employment in 2011. But this didn't last long. Less than two years later she picked up where she left off and did more UX design and project management for clients from home – and she's been going strong ever since. She's now looking to offer her clients a full agency web service "from soup to nuts."

Her daughter now suffers only mildly from asthma and allergies as a result of the pneumonia she contracted at the age of three. "Working from home has been a real blessing since I've been home during the day for most of her childhood."

Mary currently has no plans to return to full-time corporate employment.

maryshaw.net

Think of yourself as a business

A fundamental mindset shift occurred for me when I set up a company in 2007.

Set up a company

I'm from the UK so I set up an LTD (Limited Company); in the US you could set up an LLC (Limited Liability Company). It may be called something else in your part of the world.

Call it what you will, it's a company, a firm, a business. I'm talking about setting up a separate legal and financial entity. This may sound scary, boring, or obvious to you but don't worry.

If you don't want to start a company there is an alternative. In the UK, you can be a "sole trader," or in the US, you can be a "sole proprietor" – this allows you to claim expenses so you pay taxes only on profits not income. In the States, the sole proprietor option allows a business owner to deduct legitimate business expenses from their personal income tax return. They can use their social security number for this or keep things separate with an EIN (an Employer Identification Number). However, I would set up a business at the earliest opportunity.

For me, starting a company was easy. I spent a few hundred UK Pounds setting up the imaginatively titled "Rob Cubbon Ltd". As you may guess, I didn't spend long thinking of that name. And setting up a business bank account didn't take much time either.

I was working as a freelancer. Temporary employment agencies would tell me to go to a certain company on a certain day and I'd sit in a cubicle and get paid by the hour doing mind-numbingly boring jobs on a computer. Yeah, it sucked.

But this didn't suck: My income from these freelance gigs went to my company. And I could work on projects for clients from home and this income also went into the company. And when I'd employ other freelancers to work for me, buy stock images, fonts, software, phones, computers, etc., I'd pay these expenses from the company account.

This was a mindset shift: *I had a business.* I'm not like everyone else who works for a company and gets a paycheck.

Get a business bank account

The next step after incorporating (setting up a business) is getting a business bank account. Setting up a separate company account should be easy and inexpensive. I had to add some of my own personal money to it to get it going (maybe $50).

Now that you have a company account, you should pay your business expenses (phones, computers, software, etc.) out of this account and get your clients to pay into this account.

How do you get your hands on the money in your company account? In my case, I pay myself a tiny salary, something like $700/month and pay myself dividends of $10,000 or so every few months. If you can set up a modest monthly payment that you can live off (something like $1500/month maybe?) that would be better.

Always try to keep a surplus of at least 3 to 6 months running costs in the company's bank account.

Get an accountant

How you organize your business accounts and how you pay yourself will depend on the country your business is registered in. It's best to hire a freelance accountant to sort this all out for you. He or she will know how to structure the company to comply with the local tax and business legislation.

Your job is to make sure the business makes enough money to cover your business expenses and taxes, and has enough left over so that you can survive (pay your normal living expenses: rent, food, clothes, etc.). Other than that, all you have to do is to make sure the payments go into and come out of the correct accounts.

Make sure you have a PayPal business account. I have a PayPal account linked to my Yahoo! email address which I use for personal purchases and a business PayPal account linked to my *rob@robcubbon.com* business email for business expenses and income.

You may like to get a credit card for your company as well. This isn't always possible so if you have to make credit card payments you can use your personal credit card and inform your accountant about these payments.

At the end of my company's financial year it takes me less than a few hours to provide the necessary information to my accountant.

I download the business bank account comings and goings, the business PayPal account comings and goings as well as selected purchases from my personal credit card. I mark up these

Excel spreadsheets to let the accountant know what the expenses are for (stock imagery, outsourcing, web hosting, phones, computer equipment, travel and hotel stays for conferences, etc.).

There is one other spreadsheet my accountant needs and that is a list of my invoiced or billed client work. This spreadsheet consists of the date the invoice was created, the date it was paid together with the client's name, and the amount billed.

That's it. Your accountant will know exactly what to ask for so you don't need to worry about this. I never pay my accountant more than $1000 a year since he charges by the hour.

He then submits the accounts in the UK and sorts out how much company tax I have to pay. He also provides me with the figures I should include on my personal tax form, which I submit online.

Don't spend all your money

This is different from receiving a paycheck every month with the tax already paid. As an entrepreneur, it's important to set aside at least 30% of your income to pay the tax bill when it comes.

As I've already said, I've spoken to many inspiring entrepreneurs from every possible social, national, and domestic background who've all managed to make this leap and maintained their finances.

Mary Shaw, who we've already met, is one of them and she said something very wise when I interviewed her: "Every dollar you earn is really only 70 cents (or less depending on your tax bracket)."

You should always have a surplus in your bank accounts and never "run them on empty." This goes back to the minimal lifestyle we spoke about earlier. Make sure you only buy what you need.

When you are starting out, you should spend on your business according to your business's needs and regardless of short-term account surpluses. As your business grows and becomes stable, you will want to re-invest profits to grow the business further. That's different than being frugal in the early stages.

It's essential that you separate your personal and business affairs, no matter which country you are from. Without this you aren't an entrepreneur; you're a "wantrepreneur" or a dreamer.

This simple, inexpensive act changes nothing initially but it changes everything on a deep level for your life, your freedom, and your personal development. I'm not exaggerating.

But remember, business and tax laws vary from country to country so please consult a professional accountant before making any financial decisions.

The beauty and freedom of entrepreneurship

No one can tell you when to free yourself or how to do it. You can only research and meet other people who've done it and make the move yourself.

Sriranga Ramaseshan, for example, a young father born to a poor family in Bangalore, left a great job at Hewlett Packard to start up a school with 6 months savings in his back pocket. *Jyotsna Ramachandran*, another Indian, this time from Chennai, also had 6 months before she made the jump.

How much should you have saved up? I don't know because we're all different. But I hope this booklet will help you with the decision. Typically, these "runways", as they're called, are between six and twelve months.

What's the worst thing that will happen? You go back to the life that you had.

Mary Shaw did just that. The delayed effects of the 2008 financial crisis in the states hit home for her in 2011. She went back to work, impressed everybody with the skills she'd picked up from years of entrepreneurship and quit again a year later with dozens more great business contacts in her back pocket.

Mary also tells us about health insurance in the States: "You have to treat yourself the way a valued employee would be treated. You have to think about health insurance. I'm fortunate, my husband has a full-time job so we get our benefits on that side. Eventually we may have to flip-flop so that I'll provide the health insurance through my company. But it's expensive and it's rising all the time."

"As much as you have to plan for taxes you have to plan for retirement too. Here in the states, as a corporate employee you get a 401K. So I have a SEP (Simplified Employee Pension) which invests 20% of my profits."

There is a lot of difference in the needs around the world for healthcare and pensions. For example, people from the UK and Canada may be less concerned with health insurance than Americans.

You could also consider investing in a private pension scheme.

The tax situation in every country is changing all the time so PLEASE know that this advice from the interviewees and myself is NOT professional advice and you should seek professional guidance yourself.

You can mitigate your risks with insurance, pensions and savings as much as you want. The fact is: **the security of corporate employment is not what it once was.**

As an employee, you could be sacked, made redundant or forced to retire at any moment. As an entrepreneur you will experience ups and downs but you can retire or semi-retire when you want. And, with decades of business experience under your belt, you'll probably be financially secure when you decide to stop working. Or maybe you'll never want to stop working.

The scary facts for the salaried classes are all too evident. In

Western Europe and America there will be three retirees for every one working person in 20 years time. The current fiscal arrangements are not fit for people to be secure in retirement or ill health. It's better we look after ourselves and our families as best we can.

So, it seems that entrepreneurship, far from being a risky option, may be the safest way to go.

Freedom Case Study: *Using entrepreneurship to replace a multiple six-figure salary with Brian Creager*

In the early nineties, Brian had an epiphany. As a "typical engineer," (his words) working for a corporation in the plumbing space, he suddenly realized that few companies are run by engineers. So Brian took an MBA in his spare-time and moved departments from engineering to sales and marketing.

In the year 2000, he moved to another corporation, DiversiTech, a components manufacturer in the heating, ventilating, air conditioning, and refrigeration space.

He worked his way up from international sales manager to Vice President of European Sales to Vice President of Marketing. Brian was a high-flyer. He was responsible for creating new product lines and new brands, and specialized in overseas business and development. He even started two subsidiary companies in Europe. However, these companies were deemed unnecessary in one board meeting and, before Christmas 2012, Brian found himself firing three colleagues.

Telling someone you've worked closely with that they no longer had a job just before Christmas was a sobering experience.

"I'd just built two multi-million dollar companies for someone else. I stopped wanting to start products and businesses for other people," confessed Brian.

However, he was on a multi six-figure salary and had a wife and two kids (a tween and a teen). How was he going to replace that salary while supporting his family?

"Nobody goes into this knowing all the answers," he said. Meaning: you just have to *start*.

Because of his experience of getting American companies established in Europe, he dabbled in international business consulting. This proved to be a red herring.

While helping a friend set up a barber's shop, Brian had a "light bulb moment." His friend mentioned that barbers sell a lot of products in their shops. This gave him the idea for a men's hair care product.

Brian was strict with his time. He worked on his business from 3am to 7am and worked his corporate job from 8am to 5pm and put in hours on the weekends.

In February 2014, Brian had his brand (krieger + söhne®), a product, some inventory, and a website. A chance conversation with an associate at a conference prompted him to put the products on Amazon. He purchased a course to make sure he presented the product correctly in the marketplace.

Two months later, Brian had sold 30 bottles of his shampoo – $600 revenue before costs.

However, Brian's quick mastery of the Amazon marketplace

meant that, by the end of that year, his monthly gross profit exceeded his corporate income (remember he was on multiple six-figures).

But Brian still didn't leave his job. Instead, he invested the money in staff to grow his business further.

I spoke to him in August 2015 after he'd finally quit his 23-year corporate career. He was in Belgium setting up a European subsidiary. Who was helping him with that? One of the former colleagues his corporation had told him to fire before Christmas 2012.

Now he plans to build more product lines and more brands and take them to market through the Amazon platform where he has seen most success. He's confident that the business will do more than $1 million in revenue in 2015.

He's also launching his own community of entrepreneurs selling online physical products, called Zonsquad: "You never know what you're doing that will lead to something else." You've got to try a few things. It's very unlikely that you'll see success with your first idea.

Brian is now doing what he wants to do. He's taking a sabbatical and spending time with his family on extended holidays. He's enjoying what his work – creating products, brands, and making things happen. And, nobody else is telling him to fire people.

Brian left me with a great piece of advice: "Make sure you're running toward something, but also make sure not you're running away from something."

In other words: don't let your sole motivation be negative. Don't become an entrepreneur just because you hate your job. Make sure there's positivity in your motivation; become an entrepreneur because you love creating things, whatever they are. Otherwise, it won't work.

briancreager.com

www.zonsquad.com

Create that damn website

Whether you want to make "active income" by working for clients (swapping hours for dollars) or whether you want to make "passive income" by creating a product (so you can earn money in your sleep), you're going to need a website.

The best I can do at this point is to recommend an amazing book I wrote. Modest, right? It's called *Create the Website You Want with WordPress: A how-to guide for building a branded business asset.* This will tell you everything you need to know about setting up a website, making it look good, creating content on it and monetizing it. Here's a synopsis:

First, it's important to know that you can do it. You can build a successful, great-looking website relatively cheaply with little or no technical knowledge.

The second thing to realize is that you just need to do it. Register a domain, buy web hosting, set up WordPress, and get your message out there. It's as simple as that. Why? Because it's impossible to make a mistake with your own site that you can't rectify at a later date.

Choosing your domain name

The domain name is the 'something' in the 'www.something. com' of your website's address. It is also your brand.

This is the only decision I allow you to spend time thinking about. You can change your domain name at a later date but it's better to get it right first time.

Ideally, a domain name should be short, contain only letters (without hyphens, numbers or non-alphabetical symbols). I still think a dot com extension is best but I would consider others. Most importantly, pick a domain that, when spoken out loud, can be understood and people know what to type in the browser's address bar.

Adding "keywords" to the domain of a website has certain advantages. So if you want to run a web design business, for example, you could search for domains with the keywords "web design" in them. *LeanDomainSearch.com* will help with this.

However, if you put keywords into the domain of your website, it may be incongruent when you change or "pivot" your business's direction at a later date. In our "web design" example, what happens if you discover a great opportunity outside the web design niche?

You may want to go for 'neutral' words. An example of this would be QuickSprout.com, a website about SEO and online marketing. The words themselves don't have any meaning at all.

My website is RobCubbon.com – it's my first and last name. It didn't take me ages to come up with. Using your name as the domain name of your business means that you can create content about different things and it's easier to pivot the business.

Your name is easy to brand. It's you. People like doing business with people not companies.

But the decision is yours. Don't take too long making it. How do you find out if a domain is available or not? Use the search function at a domain name registrar such as GoDaddy, 123-Reg or NameCheap.

Registering your domain name should cost around $9 a year.

There are links to all the tools, apps and services mentioned in this chapter at this book's resources page: *robcubbon.com/kindle7*

Web hosting

In addition to registering a domain name, you'll have to get some web hosting.

Most domain name registrars, like GoDaddy for example, will offer hosting as well but I've always found it better to buy hosting with a different company.

There are tons of affordable webhosts out there. You get what you pay for. Very cheap web hosting is probably sufficient when you're starting out, but you may want to upgrade as your website and business grows.

Again, I will list hosts on the resources page for this booklet but I would recommend: Bluehost, Hostgator or Justhost in the US. A good host in the UK is Vidahost. A very good host but more expensive is LiquidWeb.

Inexpensive web hosting will set you back $50-100 a year, and allow you to get your site online.

Once you have a domain name and a web host you need to point the domain at the domain name registrar to the host. You can do this by like "changing NameServers" or "configuring the DNS" at your domain name registrar.

And then you're all systems go!

Setting up a Content Management System (CMS) to run your website

A Content Management System is an administrative "back-end" for your website. A place where you add the content, upload the images and organize your online presence.

If you only want a small website that's not going to be integral to your business you could use a service like SquareSpace or Wix which are inexpensive ways to put up an online "face" for your business. In fact, these easy website builders will even sort out the hosting and domain name registration for you.

However, if your website is to have any importance at all, for me, there's only one choice for a CMS: WordPress.

WordPress

WordPress is the free, open source platform that powers 20-25% of the world's websites and is the only CMS I would recommend. Most web hosts even provide an easy "one-click" service to install WordPress.

It's perfectly possible to set up WordPress at your own dot com with zero technical knowledge and I would urge you to do as much as you can yourself.

WordPress has hundreds of millions of users so every possible question about it can be answered with a Google search. And because it has become the de facto standard on which most modern websites are built, there are thousands of qualified web developers who can help you on-demand as your needs come up.

You can find them on freelance sites such as Upwork.

I have free courses on starting websites and WordPress at my site: *robcubbon.com/freecourses*

Don't worry and create content!

There's a reason why I'm rushing through this section and it's this: it doesn't matter how your website is set up and it doesn't matter how it looks. Now, don't get me wrong, in the long term you'll want a great looking website that provides a great visitor experience. But, if you're starting out, content creation is the priority on a website. And, if you already have a website, content is the most important thing.

Online, content is king. The style or design that the content is delivered in can be changed independently, Sso you it's better to have an ugly looking website with great content than a beautifully designed website with no substance.

Why this desperate need for content on your website? Because without it, you'll never know if you're offering the right information to the right audience. You may not even know who your audience is.

Your content is a conversation starter between you and your customers. The more you put out content and get feedback, the better you'll understand your market.

So what is content? Content is any information you can share that your potential audience will find helpful, valuable, or entertaining. My favorite form of content is written articles, but others have seen massive success with video (YouTube) and audio (podcast) content as well.

What do Sir Richard Branson, Seth Godin, and James Altucher have in common? They're all millionaire entrepreneurs, yes, but there's another similarity. They all regularly create free quality content. Usually every day.

If it's good enough for them it should be good enough for us.

You must regularly create useful relevant content.

What sort of content should I create?

Create useful content about what you know. You have to come from a position of authenticity. You have to be honest and know what you're talking about.

Don't write a general article about something you don't know well and just impart "wisdom" that you've read elsewhere. People can sense inauthenticity from the other side of the globe. They'll realize that this person is phony even without thinking it.

Don't worry if you don't think you know anything earth-shatteringly clever or interesting. That's the beauty of the Internet. It only has to be useful to a few people for you to start building clientele.

Think of something you learned how to do recently. You now know something you didn't know a month ago. So you could create content that would be useful to yourself a month ago, and it will undoubtedly be useful to other people as well.

So, say you are an account manager at an advertising agency. You've discovered this nifty little technique of getting people's attention on LinkedIn and it's really working for you to connect with people there. That would make a great little online article or "blog post."

Really drill into the detail and use plenty of keywords in the title. Write as much as you can. Make it entertaining. Add subheadings with keywords. Add images. Add useful downloadable materials like Word or PowerPoint documents that other people can use.

Make it as specific as possible. Why? Because the general articles will never get you noticed and, more importantly, you'll don't stand a chance of coming up in search engines if you write general broad headlines for your content.

The headline is the most important part of your content. It should both sound interesting and contain a lot of specific keywords. A good example of this is a recent blog post of mine: *Udemy Alternatives For Selling Video Courses Online.* "Udemy",

"Udemy Alternatives", "Selling Video Courses", "Video Courses Online", "Selling Video Courses Online." These are all keywords that people will search for in Google. Not many other sites had information on this subject so I could attract traffic straightaway that was interested in online learning platforms. And that's traffic I can sell to.

Install *Google Analytics* so that you can discover what your audience is thinking. After a few months, you should be able to see what people are typing into the search engines before they land on your site.

In Google Analytics, go Acquisition > Traffic > Organic Search or Acquisition > Campaigns > Organic Keywords (it's the same). Here you can see if people are searching for something that you don't have an article on. Quite often Google will send people to your site when they're searching for stuff similar to what you've already written about. This is a unique opportunity.

Not only does this show you what your audience demands, it also shows you that no one else is satisfying that demand – if there was content already catering to these keywords, Google would send traffic there instead. So create content around the keywords you're already ranking for (as long as it's something you want to offer) and you'll get even more traffic.

For example, I found that I was getting a lot of organic traffic for an old article that offered free calendars so I created a better, more up-to-date version of that article and it exploded.

You don't need to have a big site, spend money on advertising, or be linked to from authority websites. You just need to create content in very specific areas that you know a lot about. And everybody has a "sweet spot" of subject matter expertise they know lots about. Follow your interests and make your titles ultra-specific.

How do I make sure people find my website?

This is really a "billion dollar" question as the SEO (Search Engine Optimisation) industry is probably worth more than that. The answer is: **create great content and great relationships with other people in your industry**.

You cannot grow a website without content or relationships.

As I said earlier in this booklet: go out and meet *face-to-face* with as many people within your industry as possible. Try to go to as many meetups and conferences as you can. It doesn't matter if the people you meet are experts, beginners, or at the same stage of their journey as you are, as long as they're in a related industry.

When you meet these people, find out what their passions are and see if you can help them. It's possible that you know of a tool they could use to improve their business. Maybe you know someone else you could introduce them to. Go out and meet people with the mindset of helping them.

And, while helping people in the "real" or offline world, you should help people in the online world in exactly the same way. Wherever you are online – Facebook groups, LinkedIn, Google+ or forums, blog comments or email – try to help people as much as possible. (Don't spread yourself too thin. It's better to stick to a very small number of groups, maybe only 2 or 3, and get known in these groups as an authority in a subject area.)

If someone is floundering with a specific problem and you know how to help them, help them.

What on earth has this got to do with SEO? Everything. It's the best SEO tactic ever. It's nearly the only SEO tactic I've ever used!

When you help people, people are likely to help you back. And they could help you by linking to your site or promoting your business in some other way.

The machinery of business is oiled with personal relationships. And online business is no different.

I can give you an example of this happening to me. There is no better way to help business people than to help their bottom line.

Recently, I have been helping some high authority bloggers sell video courses on Udemy. Some of them reached out to me because they'd seen articles I'd written about Udemy, but others I reached out to proactively. Since I helped these influential online entrepreneurs make money, many of them linked to my Udemy articles, which are now doing very well on Google.

Links are what everyone wants. If a great site links to you, not only do you get all their traffic, but also Google sees that link as a "thumbs up" to your authority and sends even more traffic as a result. Links work even better when they're relevant. So as many high quality sites have linked to me from articles about Udemy to my articles about Udemy, Google's algorithm says to itself: "Rob's the Udemy guy!"

I also sell high-end products about Udemy, so doing a few favors for a few friends (which I was happy to do) has brought me links, traffic, and product sales.

This is only one small example of how relationships make business. Stop at nothing to create, nurture, and improve your business relationships.

How to promote your website online

The other way to make sure your website gets eyeballs is with social media. Sadly, some people concentrate on social media promotion and spend most of their day pimping their stuff online – don't be one of these people!

Social media works in the same way as online and offline relationships – **you have to give first in order to receive.** So, on Facebook, Twitter, LinkedIn, Google+, or whatever social network, be sure to post great links and great information at least three times more than you post your own stuff.

It doesn't matter if you're in LinkedIn groups, Google+ communities or Facebook groups related to your business – don't spread yourself too thin – and give, give, give before you ask someone to visit your own site.

There's one more extremely important way to promote your website and online business and it involves collecting the email addresses of your customers and potential customers. We'll cover that in the next chapter before another of our "Freedom Case Studies".

Freedom Case Study: *Starting a business and a family at the same time Jyotsna Ramachandran from Chennai, India*

At the beginning of 2012, Jyotsna Ramachandran quit her job as an area manager for Diesel in Chennai, southern India. She disliked the amount of travel the job involved and she was also bored (although the salary was good).

Her husband was an area manager in an Indian coffee chain and he fully supported her change of direction. She had saved up 6 months rent before making the jump into entrepreneurship. If things didn't work out she could always go back to work.

Using her local retail contacts she started a retail staff recruitment company. After two years, this was bringing in $1000-1500/month.

Becoming pregnant caused another change in Jyotsna's life. Suddenly she didn't feel able to go to meetings and run a brick and mortar business. She started to look around for online opportunities.

After taking a course on self-publishing on Amazon's Kindle

platform, Jyotsna began publishing ghost-written Kindle books. She'd published 10 by the time her daughter was one year old. These were bringing in $400-500/month.

A year later, Jyotsna finally sat down to write a book of her own. Within two months she had finished *The Job Escape Plan*, which was an instant bestseller on Amazon. It's a very similar book to this one and, if you haven't already, I would urge you to read it.

In May 2015 she had her most successful month on Kindle, with earnings from her full portfolio of titles topping $5300.

jyotsnaramachandran.com

Turning website visitors into customers

Every website should have a purpose. Sometimes a website's purpose will be to sell products. Sometimes it will be to educate, inform, or entertain. Your website's purpose, initially, may well be to get potential clients to contact you.

Getting clients online

Remember I told you that web page titles are important? The title of my home page (therefore the title of my site) used to be "Freelance Graphic Designer London". The reason for this was that I was trying to rank for those keywords.

I put myself in the shoes of a potential client and wondered what they'd type into Google to find someone like me. I figured that "Freelance Graphic Designer London" were buying keywords.

I wrote multiple blog posts with the words "Freelance Graphic Designer London" in the title and got links from other design-related websites. This meant that whenever someone searched for "Freelance Graphic Designer London" I ranked amongst the first few websites that came up.

I didn't do anything extra on the site – no huge banner saying "HIRE ME!" Just a contact link in the top navigation bar of the site to a page with my email address, phone number, and contact form.

I got hundreds of clients this way.

Can you think of buying keywords to sum up what you do? Think of your target market and the one thing you want them to do when they arrive at the website. See if you can think of keywords that your target market would key in to Google.

Why you should collect email addresses from your website

Your website is NOT your most important online asset. That honor is reserved for your email list.

When I say "email list" I'm not talking about your contacts in Gmail or Outlook. Your email list is a collection of email addresses from people who've visited your website.

If you have a website but don't have an email list you need to stop reading right now and go to AWeber, MailChimp, or ActiveCampaign and set up an account. I'm not joking. It's that important. It's also free when you start.

Email is not just your most effective means of online promotion (making money), it is also your most effective means of researching into your customers and potential customers.

Just imagine being able to communicate directly with the people in the world who are more interested in your business than anyone else? Whether you have an email list of 40 people, 400 people, or 4,000 people, that's who they are: the 40, 400, or 4,000 people in the world who are more likely to buy products or services from you than anybody else.

How you should collect email addresses from your website

Again, think of your target market. What could you give them for free?

For example, if you're a personal trainer, you could give away a weekly training routine for free as a PDF. If you're an accountant, you could offer a free Excel spreadsheet with tax calculation macros. If you're a hypnotherapist, you could supply a free relaxation MP3.

It could be a video course, an e-book, or some software.

These freebies are called "lead magnets" or "bribes" that are offered in exchange for a prospect's email address. The people who are most interested in this offer and have no problem giving you their email address would be the same people that will eventually buy your products or services.

Think of some high value digital file that you can give away for free and offer that as your lead magnet.

None of us like being sold to. None of us like getting too much email. And we hate spam even more.

People who join your email list know they're going to get emails from you but they put up with that hassle because they believe the benefit they get from you will outweigh the disadvantages. That's why it's important to treat these people well when you email them.

Always provide value to your email list. Make sure you send at least two or three "value" emails for every sales email. And the sales emails should ideally be offers of discounted prices for limited time periods. These work best.

Always be emailing your email list – at least every two weeks. Never leave your email subscribers out in the cold. If months go by without hearing from you, they'll probably forget who you are in the first place.

Engage with your audience personally

The bigger the list, the better. So you should start collecting email addresses **now**.

But you can do *so much* with a smaller list. If you've only just started collecting email addresses then your list is very "hot" or responsive. You can ask them questions like, "What are you struggling with right now?" This is the most powerful question you can ask an email list because you'll get back vital information about your customers.

If you get the same answer again and again, create and sell a product or service that provides a solution to their struggles.

You can also contact your initial subscribers personally and offer them a free 15-minute Skype conversation. This will give you more vital information about your market. You can even take notes and copy the exact language they use. If you mimic your customers' language on sales pages, they will convert better.

Freedom Case Study: *Leaving a well-paid corporate job with Sriranga Ramaseshan from Bangalore, India*

"My parents were not financially comfortable. My father had a very basic level government job. We were very poor by Indian standards. We could only afford food and rent – we didn't own our own house. We couldn't afford any nice food or snacks. We always got public transport as we had no vehicle."

Sriranga ("Ranga") always wanted something else for himself and his family. He had a newspaper route in high school, and supported his college education (a B'Com in Commerce at Bangalore University) by working at a market research

agency part time. His degree from Bangalore University would have been enough to get Ranga a call center job, joining the ranks of thousands and thousands of Indians and others in Asia who work in BPO (Business process outsourcing).

Ranga "didn't want an ordinary level job" so he enrolled in the Institute of Chartered Accountants of India (ICAI) to study corporate and Forex accounting. This involved four years of very hard study and poorly paid internships at the Bangalore offices of large international companies. However, this qualified him for his "dream job" as a Financial Analyst at Hewlett-Packard. Ranga could now afford to move his parents into a new comfortable house. Within a year, Ranga got married and moved into his own house with a mortgage – the payments were a massive 70% of his monthly salary.

For many people this would be the end of the story. With a good job and a large mortgage, most would continue within this company for decades in order to pay off the mortgage and enjoy the benefits of a high level employment in a large international company. But Ranga was barely three months into this new "dream job" before he realized the 9 to 5 was not for him. Even though it paid well, he wasn't being challenged. Despite the burden of their mortgage, he and his wife made the decision to pursue a different path. Two and a half years later, they'd saved up enough money to be able to live and pay their bills for a year. He handed his notice in to Hewlett-Packard in March 2013. He was 27 and his wife was five months pregnant.

Now Sriranga Ramaseshan is the founder director of Eduplot Learning Solutions. He employs 20-25 teachers in his school teaching accounting qualifications. It will shortly be offering the UK (ACCA) and US (CMA) qualifications as well as the CA, ICWA, & CS, which are the major professional accounting courses in India. Getting the initial students through the door may have been challenging at first, but Ranga drew from his contacts and advertised in newspapers and universities. His school is now educating the next generation of graduates from

Bangalore who want to better themselves – just like he did. He helps students by accepting installments for course fees. He even provides free education to poor students who can demonstrate great interest in their education. This is on the school's website: "It has been the legacy of mankind to pass on the candle of knowledge and illuminate young minds." He's also passionate about online business so he is branching out into online education.

We are now in 2015, two years after Ranga quit his safe, well-paying job with HP. He has successfully replaced his corporate salary with the proceeds from the business. His daughter is two years old.

www.linkedin.com/in/srirangar
www.eduplot.com

Action steps

It's my hope that this book will help you in some way. Information is essential to achieve freedom in your life. However, the one thing more important than information is **action**.

You have to take action if you're going to do this. And yet we find action so hard to take sometimes. We become so paralyzed with questions we end up doing nothing.

What's the antidote to this "analysis paralysis"? Action, action, and then, more action.

Even if the action takes you in the wrong direction, you'll learn something new. In business, action is never a waste of time.

I'm going to set out some action steps you can take to help free yourself from employment.

Think for five minutes about your "sweet spot"

The sweet spot is a magical place where your passion, what you're good at, and what you can get paid for all intersect.

Everyone's got a sweet spot – just like everyone's got a heart.

I found my sweet spot through taking action. I created content around what I was doing in employment and started earning money doing that. It wasn't necessarily magic right out of the gate, but it was good enough for me.

Later, after successfully running a graphic design business, I honed in on an even sweeter spot; helping people start businesses and find clients.

So spend five minutes on this but no longer. Don't worry if you don't think you've honed in on an amazing sweet spot. You will find your sweet spot through action.

Decide on a domain name

A domain name can quite often be a sticking point. People usually spend way too much time thinking about it.

Try *LeanDomainSearch.com* or, better still, just buy a domain with your name in it. If you have a common name like John Smith, try something like TheRealJohnSmith.com. You can also see what's available in .net, .io, or other domain "extensions." The advantage of using your real name in the domain is that you can pivot or change your business slightly and it'll still fit in with the domain.

Make the decision quickly. It's not that important and you can always change it later (although that is a bit of a hassle).

Set up a website

People get really hung up on the design of their site and various other things. But it's the site's content and authority that is important. The longer a site has been around, the more authority it has, so it's better to start today.

It doesn't need to look amazing at first, but the content and keywords it has on it are important.

I have some free step-by-step instructions on how to do this here: *robcubbon.com/kindle7*

Start collecting emails

If you haven't started collecting emails yet you should do it now. Go to MailChimp, ActiveCampaign, or AWeber and set up an account.

Put a sign up form on your website. This may only take you five minutes and it is perhaps the most important element of your website.

If you've already started collecting emails, contact a few of your subscribers personally and ask them what they are struggling with.

Do you have an auto-responder sequence yet? This is a series of email messages that gets sent automatically to new subscribers. Every few days you can send them some more helpful information, which helps them get to know you better and builds trust. In the first message in your sequence, include the question again: "What are you struggling with right now? Reply to this email and I'll try to help."

Further on in the sequence, maybe the second or third email, you can offer your subscribers a free 15-minute Skype consultation. Free consultations can lead to paid consulting, and they can also help with content and product ideas.

Think for five minutes about what differentiates you from others

We'd all like that niche that everyone knows us for: "I'm the auto-responder guy;" "I'm the Facebook ad lady;" "I'm the logo designer dude." But sadly, we don't all fit so well in a pigeonhole.

Can you think of a niche for yourself? If you're a designer, can you specialize in some aspect of design? If you're a writer, can you specialize in some form of writing you particularly enjoy?

If you can't, don't worry. It'll come. Spend five minutes thinking, but no more!

Write a piece of content

Writing makes you a happier person for a variety of reasons. If you write a piece of content for your website, it'll make you happier for the simple fact you'll have done something beneficial for your business.

More content gives you more authority in your niche. And every time you create content, you become a better content creator.

So create that content! Write about what you know about. Create content around what you've done this week. Be honest, be yourself and be specific!

Make a video

In addition to the published text, video is extremely powerful. Video puts you in front of your customers in a way the written word will never be able to.

If you're camera shy, you could film a short five-minute presentation using screen-casting software such as Camtasia or Screenflow and upload it to YouTube.

It probably won't be a viral sensation on YouTube, but it's a start. The next video you make will be better. You'll get used to being in front of the camera. Sooner or later you'll make a video that gets thousands and thousands of views, which will give you an advantage over your competition.

Interview someone

Try to connect with a businessperson who is further along the journey than you. You can use the questions and answers from this interview for content on your site.

You will benefit from talking to this expert. You can ask him a question about your own business. Or dress the question up so it doesn't sound selfish: "What advice would you give to someone starting out in this business now?"

Make sure you do a favor for the person you are talking to. For example, regularly share their content on social media.

WHEN YOU TALK, YOU ARE ONLY REPEATING WHAT YOU ALREADY KNOW.

BUT IF YOU *LISTEN*, YOU MAY *LEARN* SOMETHING NEW.

dalai lama

Rob Cubbon

I hope this book has helped you take action.

If it has, please consider leaving a review on Amazon. Or head along over to my site to say hi: *robcubbon.com*

I'd wanted to write this book for a long time. It's a book about freedom. About escaping. Essentially, it's about making enough money on the side to eventually leave your job and become a full time entrepreneur.

How am I qualified to write this book? Well, I did this in 2006-8. But, I never really had a proper job before that, I don't have kids to pay for and I never used to spend much money in the first place.

So I looked for people who made a scarier jump than I did. People who did it more recently, people who had been well-paid in their corporate gig and who maybe had bigger overheads (mortgage, kids, etc.), and people who were from a less privileged background than me.

I had no problem finding them.

I posted one status update on Facebook and they contacted me in their droves. These amazing people were keen to spread good news on self-employment as well as to outline the potential pitfalls.

I keep mentioning these inspiring interviews. I make no apologies for this – these people were truly amazing to talk to. Here's the last of our interviews, sadly. Meet June Bui from Vietnam.

Freedom Case Study: *Starting a life of entrepreneurship in Vietnam with June Bui*

When she was 16, June Bui (in Vietnamese, Bùi Thi Dung) moved from a poor village in the middle of Vietnam down to Ho Chi Minh City (formerly Saigon).

June did well at school and went to the prestigious Foreign Trade University and graduated with a degree in International Business Administration.

Two years after graduating, she was working in a language center where, after having achieved much in her career there, she was exposed to the growing ranks of "digital nomads" – people who are traveling the world while working online. June was hugely inspired by the freedom of time and location that the nomads enjoyed and resolved to leave her job immediately.

As a result of her university education and her work in the language center, June speaks excellent English. She was immediately able to earn money teaching English on a freelance basis.

In her spare time, she began to research more creative opportunities. She is completing illustration and design tasks for friends, family, and ex-colleagues. She has also been working through freelance sites such as Upwork, although the nature of the work there has been challenging.

Southeast Asian culture, and Vietnamese culture in particular, attaches great imance to the working a "good, stable job." However, June's family is totally supportive of her jorney towards freedom and entrepreneurship. She also has at least four friends who are exploring a similar path.

www.junillustration.tumblr.com

Conclusion

One of the main points of this book is to get you to take action.

Remember, follow your interests. Try to find something you're good at, you enjoy, that people will pay you for. Earn active income (swapping hours for dollars) first whilst preparing for passive income later.

Whatever you do, make sure you regularly create valuable free content through your own website as this'll earn you trust that you will be able to capitalize on in the future.

Always look after your mental, physical, and spiritual health and don't work at the expense of the people around you.

Make sure you're doing it for the right reasons. Become free and work for yourself because you love it.

Thank you!

Thank you so much for reading my book.

What could be better than doing something you love every day?

I love helping people with their businesses. Nothing would make me happier than if this book helped you.

Maybe you felt inspired to start your own brand and business website. Maybe you already have a business or a website and this has helped you in some way.

If so, then please consider leaving a review at Amazon. Positive reviews really help get the message out there and I'd be extremely grateful if you would pen an honest review and tell me what you thought about the book.

If you have any questions please pop along to *my website* at *robcubbon.com* and leave a comment on one of the articles or drop me a line. And remember, you can *sign up to my email list* to receive free newsletters, Kindles, and e-books. Sign up here: *robcubbon.com/free*

Cheers,

Rob Cubbon

P.S. Keep reading, there are loads more ways I can help you!

Videos and books

Video courses

I have been making various video courses for the last two years. They are on the subjects of web design, running an online business, and online marketing generally. You can join my membership site and view all these courses. You can find all these courses at *robcubbon.com/courses-overview*

Business: *Make Money Running A Web Design Business*
How to make money by running a successful web design business from home and charging 4-figures plus for every website. How to set up a business, how to find clients and how to run the business successfully.

WordPress (advanced): *Creating a Web Design Business Website*
Learn how to design and develop this site – *Crea8iveDesigns.com* – the website of a fictitious design company.

Marketing & Promotion: *Build My Brand: Blogging, SEO, Social Media & Relationships*
This course shows you how to get noticed online with blogging, social media, SEO and by building win-win relationships with other business people in your niche. It proves the success of this model by ranking for buying keywords on a new site.

Free course: *Talking To Clients: An Introduction To Website Building*

Learn how to talk to a new client. This course shows me talking to Nura Nash about her new website.

WordPress (intermediate): *Create A Custom Responsive WordPress Website For A Client*

Learn how to create this website NuraHNash.com with WordPress and the Genesis theme framework.

Free course: Email Marketing: *How To Build an Email List of Customers*

Step-by-step instructions on how to collect emails, create a relationship with your subscribers and grow your business.

You can view all these courses at *robcubbon.com/courses-overview* or, just the free courses, at *robcubbon.com/freecourses*

Other books I've written

I have also written some other booklets that have been very well reviewed, I'm pleased to say.

The first book is called *Running A Web Design Business From Home: How To Find and Keep Good Clients and Make Money with Your Home Business* – a bit of a mouthful.

The book explains how to set up your business from home – the hardware and software you'll need. I also write about how you get long term, quality clients who will recommend you and give you ongoing work. We also talk about how to run web design projects as well as the diversification of your business going forward.

It's not a "get rich quick" book. You are encouraged to start in your spare time and slowly but surely build up your long-term professional contacts and online authority. This will provide you with a solid base for whatever you want to achieve with your online business in the future.

Here's what one reviewer said: *I love how simply Rob explains everything. I've taken a few of his e-courses, and jumped on this book when it came out. It's a quick-read, but extremely useful. Rob does a great job of skipping the fluff and getting to the point--while keeping it interesting and upbeat. Even though I've been running my own web design company for two years now, Rob's tips are great and he gave me some great ideas to put into practice!*

If you're in the UK you can get *Running A Web Design Business From Home here*: *www.amazon.co.uk/dp/B00G5IV01Y*

If you're in the US you can get *Running A Web Design Business From Home here*: *www.amazon.com/dp/B00G5IV01Y*

And here's another book I've written that may be of interest:

How To Sell Video Courses Online

Full title: *How To Sell Video Courses Online: How I make $2000+ passive income every month*

I make over $2000 passive income every month from video tutorials and you can too.

This book explains: how to research the content and title of your courses, technical information about video course creation, advice on how to create your first course, how to market your course, and loads more.

The world is changing. Education is changing. There is a HUGE demand for career skills courses online.

Once you have created a course, it can earn you substantial money every month for years to come.

Plus you will enjoy the process of making the course and the feedback from the students. Course creation is not only very satisfying it also helps builds your brand as an authority within your niche.

Here's a review: *In all his books and blog articles, Rob Cubbon's writing reflects his down-to-earth honesty, superb clarit,y and considerable experience. In this work, Rob shows us how to record video courses once, make them available on the Internet, and earn a passive income from them for months or years afterwards. As an online instructor for nearly five years myself, I was not only informed, I was also inspired. For anyone who loves to teach, I highly recommend this powerful little book.*

If you're in the UK you can get *How To Sell Video Courses Online* here: *http://www.amazon.co.uk/dp/B00H2OEDDM/*

If you're in the US you can get *How To Sell Video Courses Online* here: *http://www.amazon.com/dp/B00H2OEDDM/*

Isn't that wonderful! I deeply appreciate all the reviews I get. If you've enjoyed this book, it would be great if you could give me a review. I would be so, so grateful.

Build a Brand, Create Products and Earn Passive Income

This is a blueprint for **online success**. It's everything I've learned during a decade of living online.

This is not a get-rich-quick book. However, if you do what it says, you will make money online.

You will also grow an authoritative personal brand that will benefit both you and your businesses for years to come.

I'm going to tell you how to enjoy creating regular content that will be consumed by a growing community of adoring fans and how to unlock the secrets of social media and email marketing to ask them what they want. And then, how to create products (books, podcasts, videos) to sell to them and others.

So, to recap: Your brand is followed by an audience. They tell you what they want, you build it, and they buy it. And you keep going. It's very simple.

And there's more good news: you won't have to spend any money.

At the end, I'm going to send you on your way with my strategy ingrained in your mind. This will help you to build your brand, create products and earn passive income. Plus you'll be able to keep going. My strategy ensures there's always more in the tank to give. Creativity breeds creativity.

You will enjoy creating content. So, let's get going!

Buy **Build a Brand, Create Products and Earn Passive Income** in the US here: *www.amazon.com/dp/B00LTWLSE0*

Buy **Build a Brand, Create Products and Earn Passive Income** in the UK here: *www.amazon.co.uk/dp/B00LTWLSE0*

From Freelancer to Entrepreneur: Escaping work and finding happiness

This is a semi-autobiographical book about how I was lost professional, emotionally and spiritually and how, bit by bit, I was able to set up my own business and work from home – with a few ups and downs along the way.

You can buy this book on Amazon US: From Freelancer to Entrepreneur: Escaping work and finding happiness *www.amazon.com/dp/B00J7BK4MC/*

You can buy this book on Amazon UK: From Freelancer to Entrepreneur: Escaping work and finding happiness *www.amazon.co.uk/dp/B00J7BK4MC*

Free Your Thoughts: How I Re-programmed Myself For Happiness And How You Can Too

This booklet will add more freedom and happiness to your life. It could change your life too.

"If you want to break free and live life on your terms, while doing work that makes a difference and adds value to other people's lives. Then you should read this book." SA – verified purchase review.

We are all freer than we think we are. But sometimes when you get up for work in the morning, freedom seems like a privilege reserved for the rich and famous. It isn't. The freest people in the world aren't usually rich or famous. This book will show you how you can experience freedom now!

This book explains the mindset shift you need **to enjoy a life of freedom and happiness**. This book contains:

- A focus on the present as the only reality we have
- A "we are capable of anything" approach
- Encouragement to evaluate your true purpose and directions on how to do that
- Explains how you are the experience and not the

experiencer
- Show you what it means to label things, and how to catch negative thinking before it turns into limiting beliefs
- Directions on how to stop judging
- Teaches the easy way to meditate
- Guidance on affirmations and how to make them work; turning affirmations into a positive statements that focus on helping people

I used to do unsatisfying jobs and not have any aspirations that my life could ever be any different.

It never occurred to me to question what I was doing and why I wasn't free to do what I wanted.

I kept on going to those boring offices to do unfulfilling work, day after day, week after week, month after month, year after year.

Now, I've just got back from a eight-month long vacation where I was travelling through Thailand, Cambodia, Vietnam and the Philippines whilst working on my online business.

How did I turn my life around? Well, every journey starts with a single step and the first step was the mindset shift which is explained in this book.

You will learn about how to create a new mindset that is positive, creative and energetic.

After reading this book you will be able control your thoughts in order to concentrate on the most important things – your life, your loves, your calling.

You can buy this book on Amazon US: *www.amazon.com/dp/B00YUY4WYM*

You can buy this book on Amazon UK: *www.amazon.co.uk/*

dp/B00YUY4WYM

Free Yourself, Leave Your Job and Be Your Own Boss

By Rob Cubbon

Copyright 2015, Rob Cubbon

All Rights Reserved

Published By:

Rob Cubbon Ltd

RobCubbon.com

Legal Disclaimer:

this report.

The author and publisher reserve the right to make any changes they deem necessary to future versions of the publication to ensure its accuracy.

The reader assumes all responsibility for the use of the information within this report.

If you do not accept the terms of this agreement, please return the product immediately for a full refund, at which point you must destroy any copies of the publication in your possession.

Peace and love!

www.ingramcontent.com/pod-product-compliance
Lightning Source LLC
Chambersburg PA
CBHW072255200526
45168CB00016B/1951